GORDON GOODWIN'S

BIG Phat BAND *Play-Along* Series

Volume 2

DRUMS

CUSTOM MIX

SYSTEM REQUIREMENTS

Windows
7, Vista, XP
1.8 GHz processor or faster
510 MB hard drive space, 2 GB RAM minimum
Speakers or headphones
Internet access required for updates
QuickTime 7.6.7 or higher

Macintosh
OS 10.4 and higher (Intel only)
620 MB hard drive space, 2 GB RAM minimum
Speakers or headphones
Internet access required for updates
QuickTime 7.6.7 or higher

Stream or download the audio & software content for this book.
To access online media, visit: **alfred.com/redeem**

Enter the following code:

00-42587-69427840

alfred.com

ISBN-10: 1-4706-1136-8
ISBN-13: 978-1-4706-1136-1

Photographs by Rex Bullington, Gary Reber, and Joe Meyer
Engineering/mixing/editing Gordon Goodwin's master tracks, Mike Aarvold
Solo transcriptions for alto sax, tenor sax, trumpet, and trombone by Benny Golbin
Solo transcriptions for Bernie Dresel's drum solos by Hal Rosenfeld

CONTENTS

Check out the full-version CD Recordings of Gordon Goodwin's Big Phat Band.

Visit: www.gordongoodwin.com

How to use the TnT2 Custom Mix Software

1. Listen to the full band and your part (mute the click track).

2. Play along with the Big Phat Band by muting *your* part (mute the click track if desired).

3. Learn the tunes by listening, and then by playing along.

4. Listen to, play, and practice the sample solos, and then solo over the chord progressions.

5. Loop sections, while slowing down or speeding up the tempo.

Introduction

There's nothing better than playing music with your friends. As a young musician, we'd get together and jam almost every day.

What a blast that was! Those early sessions were a crucial component that helped me learn and grow as a musician.

And yet, at some point, you'll hit the wall if playing with the same group of guys all the time; the very thing that makes you comfortable as friends may stunt your musical growth. Your most significant growth will happen when you put yourself in new situations and play music with new people. And the most noteworthy progress happens when those new people are better than you. It's not as fun at the time, but sitting down next to someone who can musically carve you up—that's how you get better. And it can happen quickly!

The main goal of this play-along series is to teach the art of ensemble playing. You will learn volumes of information about style, phrasing, tone, dynamics, technique, articulation, playing in time, Latin grooves, funk grooves, swing grooves, and more. This play-along series provides a virtual environment in which the player/student can sit next to some of the best musicians in the business, the members of the Big Phat Band.

Describing the Phat Band musicians in that way may seem like hyperbole, but I've seen what these guys can do night after night. They play with a high level of consistency and excellence, regardless of the style and difficulty level. And it doesn't stop with their technical mastery of the material; they also routinely elevate the music to a *higher* level, beyond the notes on the page. Participating in this series are five outstanding musicians from the band. They are all world-class performers, and their guidance will be invaluable as you dig into this music.

So, this is your great opportunity and challenge, as well—to sit down next to Wayne Bergeron, or Eric Marienthal, or Andy Martin, or Brian Scanlon, or Bernie Dresel, and hold down your chair. Show 'em you belong! Some of the music in this book is definitely a challenge. But I would encourage you to avoid characterizing music as "easy" or "hard." These terms are self-limiting. Take things as they come, do your best, and stick to it. Progress comes a step at a time. But that brings us to another point about using this book.

Learning to be efficient in your practice time is a valuable skill. Set goals for each practice session and work on material *that you cannot play well*, not stuff that already sounds good. Practice, at least in this sense, is not performance. Many things are common to both practice and performance, including commitment, focus, and energy. However, I suggest you pick something you want to improve, and in a deliberate, surgical manner, set about to perfect it. When you fire up the TNT 2 tracks in your computer, the band will start cooking, and the tendency will be to blow! While this is fun, you don't want to skip over licks in the music that may need work.

And here is where Alfred's TNT 2 software comes in. In addition to many other features, this amazing program allows you to change the tempo of the track without altering the pitch. Slow the tempo down to accommodate a phrase, get that lick in shape, and then crank that tempo up again! This valuable tool helps you become comfortable playing at a variety of tempos. Use it wisely!

Since improvisation is an important facet in jazz, the saxophone, trumpet, and trombone books all have chord changes for the solo sections. The online tracks have the solos mixed out so that you can jump in and blow! I highly suggest you check out and learn from the transcriptions of some of the improvised solos found on the Big Phat Band recordings and included in these books. You can use these transcribed solos to study, practice as études, or simply play in the solo sections of each respective track. On the drum book disk, the original horn solos have been kept intact so you can play off the soloist.

To get the most from the play-along audio, you can, of course, use headphones as you play along with the tracks. But for me, the most realistic acoustical environment involves listening to the music through speakers with your ears unhindered by headphones. The key is to be able to hear yourself as well as everybody else in the band, and playing with headphones can make it tricky to get the balance right.

We have a policy in the Big Phat Band. On our gigs, we come to play—every night. We work hard, we make no excuses, and we go for it, all the while having a blast. We never lose sight of the fact that playing music together is a gift not to be taken for granted. I hope you will bring those qualities to mind as you work with this book, and that it helps you grow as a musician.

—Gordon Goodwin
www.gordongoodwin.com

Gordon Goodwin

Even for a successful composer and arranger in Hollywood, Gordon Goodwin's numbers are impressive: a 2006 GRAMMY® Award for his instrumental arrangement of "Incredits" from the Pixar film *The Incredibles*, three Emmy® Awards, and fourteen GRAMMY nominations, including a 2012 GRAMMY Award for his arrangement of George Gershwin's "Rhapsody in Blue."

Here's another impressive number to add to the list: eighteen. As in the number of musicians in Gordon Goodwin's Big Phat Band, one of the most exciting large jazz ensembles on the planet. Populated by L.A.'s finest players, the Big Phat Band takes the big band tradition into the new millennium with a contemporary, highly original sound featuring Goodwin's witty, intricate, and hard-swinging compositions in a veritable grab bag of styles: swing, Latin, blues, classical, rock, and more.

A steady, persistent audio diet of the giants of jazz, pop, rock, and funk has nourished Goodwin's being since childhood. Count Basie, Duke Ellington, Buddy Rich, Thad Jones and Mel Lewis, Earth, Wind & Fire, and Tower of Power, among many others, filled the well for the music his band makes today. And like those other bands, Goodwin is nothing less than astonishing when experienced live.

A keyboardist and woodwind player, Goodwin has built a larger-than-life reputation throughout the music industry for his composing, arranging, and playing skills. Ray Charles, Christina Aguilera, Johnny Mathis, Toni Braxton, John Williams, Natalie Cole, David Foster, Sarah Vaughan, Mel Tormé, Brian McKnight, and Quincy Jones are just a few of the artists with whom he has worked. Goodwin has also conducted world-renowned symphony orchestras in Atlanta, Dallas, Utah, Seattle, Toronto, and London.

Goodwin's ability to combine jazz excellence with any musical style makes his writing appealing to fans across the spectrum. That's why both beboppers and headbangers dig Gordon Goodwin's Big Phat Band.

CD, Album, and DVD Releases

- *Swingin' for the Fences*, featuring guest artists Arturo Sandoval and Eddie Daniels (Silverline Records, 2000)

- *XXL*, featuring, among others, Johnny Mathis and Michael Brecker (Silverline Records, 2003)
- *The Phat Pack*, with guest stars Dianne Reeves, David Sanborn, Eddie Daniels, and Take 6 (Immergent Records, 2008)
- *Act Your Age*, produced by acclaimed guitarist Lee Ritenour and featuring a host of notable guests, including Patti Austin, Chick Corea, Dave Grusin, and Ritenour himself, plus a special appearance by the late pianist Art Tatum (Immergent Records, 2006)
- *That's How We Roll*, including special guests Gerald Albright, Dave Koz, Marcus Miller, and Take 6 (Telarc International, 2011)
- *Life in the Bubble* (expected in 2014)

Notable Film Scoring and Orchestration

- *The Sorcerer's Apprentice* (Walt Disney Pictures, 2010)
- *Get Smart* (Warner Bros., 2008)
- *Glory Road* (Disney, 2006)
- *National Treasure* (Walt Disney Pictures, 2004)
- *The Incredibles* (Walt Disney Pictures, 2004)
- *Remember the Titans* (Jerry Bruckheimer Films, 2000)
- *Armageddon* (Touchstone Pictures, 1998)
- *The Majestic* (Castle Rock Entertainment, 2001)
- *Con Air* (Touchstone Pictures, 1997)
- *Gone in Sixty Seconds* (Buena Vista Home Entertainment, 2000)
- *Enemy of the State* (Touchstone Pictures, 1998)
- *Star Trek: Nemesis* (Paramount Pictures, 2002)
- *Bah Humduck! A Looney Tunes Christmas* (Warner Bros., 2006)

Gordon Goodwin's Acknowledgments

The content in this book is the result of the efforts of a large number of talented people. I am indebted to them all, but especially:

- The musicians in the Big Phat Band. You've heard 'em. They are amazing, each and every time they play.
- My co-producers on the Big Phat Band releases *That's How We Roll* and *Life in the Bubble*, Gregg Field and Dan Savant. There's nothing better than making music with your good friends.
- Pete BarenBregge, my editor at Alfred Music, whose knowledge and energy seems never to cease. A truly valuable ally.
- My wife Lisa and kids Madison, Trevor, and Garrison have long lived their lives in the "Phat Lane" and are the best ever. Love them.
- My mom Alice Goodwin, who drove me to piano lessons, and you know, got everything rolling. Love her, too—so would you.
- The Concord Music Group, our record label, who continue to fight the good fight in bringing music of quality to our beleaguered culture.
- Tommy Vicari and Gregg Field, whose audio recording and mixing skills are unmatched in the industry. And Mike Aarvold, who expertly prepared the complicated audio mixes for this book.
- My manager Kevin Raleigh, who probably had no idea what he was getting into when he signed on! Too late now, pal.

Bernie Dresel

Bernie Dresel has occupied the challenging drum chair for the GRAMMY-nominated Gordon Goodwin Big Phat Band since its inception in 1999. And for an overlapping 15 years (1992–2006), he was the drummer for the GRAMMY-winning Brian Setzer Orchestra. *Modern Drummer* magazine's Readers Poll named him "Best Big Band Drummer" and *Drum! Magazine* has put him on their list of "53 Drummers Who Made a Difference in the 90s" as well as honoring him with a 2002 "Drummie" award for Best Big Band Drummer.

Bernie is also busy with Los Angeles session work as a versatile drummer and percussionist. He has recorded and performed with many performers such as: the Brian Setzer Orchestra, 68 Comeback Special, Brian Setzer Trio, Brian Setzer and the Nashvillains, Gordon Goodwin's Big Phat Band, Carl Verheyen, Cecilia Noel and the Wild Clams, Men at Work, Andy Summers, James Taylor, James Brown, Frank Sinatra, Frank Sinatra, Jr., Jack Jones, Andrea Bocelli, Alf Clausen Jazz Orchestra, Chaka Khan, Ringo Starr, Little Richard, Brian Wilson, David Byrne, Dr. John, Albert Lee, Gene Simmons, B.B. King, Patti LaBelle, Brian Adams, Luis Miguel, Petula Clark, Lesley Gore, Gwen Stefani, Christina Aguilera, Steven Van Zandt, Chris Isaak, Paula Abdul, Joe Strummer, Hootie & the Blowfish, Babyface, Celine Dion, David Foster, Vanessa Williams, Natalie Cole, Brenda Russell, Carl Anderson, Marietta Waters, Ellis Hall, Ann Margret, Julie Andrews, Ray Charles, Linda Ronstadt, Gloria Estefan, James Ingram, Smokie Robinson, George Clinton, Walter Murphy, Nancy Wilson, Stevie Wonder, Peabo Bryson, Roberta Flack, Tom Jones, Maynard Ferguson, Clare Fischer, Diane Reeves, Robben Ford, Lee Ritenour, The Rippingtons, Patti Austin, Arturo Sandoval, Lou Rawls, Barry Manilow, Gloria Loring, Steve Lawrence and Eydie Gorme, Shelby Flint, Marilyn Scott, Carl Anderson, Ben Vereen, Michael Crawford, Lea Salonga, Shirley MacLaine, Bill Elliott Swing Orchestra, Chris Walden Big Band, Buddy Childers Big Band, Bob Florence Big Band, LeAnn Rimes, Johnny Hallyday, Sylvie Vartan, Carlos De Antonis, Hotei, Yukari Ito, Nick Lachey, Liel, Billy Gilman, Thelma Houston, Expose, Mila, Randy Newman, Trevor Rabin, Johnny Mandel, the Dixie Chicks, Hannah Montana, the Jonas Brothers, and of course, BERN!

Bernie has performed on movie soundtracks as well: *Mission: Impossible – Ghost Protocol, Man of Steel, John Carter, New Year's Eve, Cars 2, Jersey Boys, Super 8, Mr. Popper's Penguins, Transformers: Dark of the Moon, Get on Up, Monte Carlo, Charlie St. Cloud, Marmaduke, Up, Star Trek (2009), Mars Needs Moms, Speed Racer, The Bourne Supremacy, Payback, Hulk, Ratatouille, Rapunzel, The Princess and the Frog, The Country Bears, Star Trek: Generations, Pearl Harbor, Private Parts, A Thousand Words, Foodfight!, Soldier, A Dirty Shame, Higher Learning*, and many more.

In addition, Dresel has performed the music for many television shows including: *Family Guy, American Dad, The Simpsons, King of the Hill, Pinky and the Brain, Animaniacs, Tiny Toon Adventures, Scooby-Doo, Where Are You!, Road Rovers, Mickey Mouse Works, The Sopranos, Bones, Jag, Star Trek: Voyager, Star Trek: The Next Generation, Star Trek: Deep Space Nine, Star Trek: Enterprise, Jake and the Fatman, The Young Indiana Jones Chronicles, Dawson's Creek, Baywatch, The Young and the Restless, Passions, General Hospital, The American Music Awards, The Golden Globe Awards, The Screen Actors Guild Awards®, The Emmy Awards®, The American Comedy Awards, Quincy Jones…The First 50 Years, Sinatra: 80 Years My Way, Dallas, Knots Landing, Simon & Simon, Murder, She Wrote, Diagnosis Murder, Newhart, Cheers, Suddenly Susan, The Nanny, It's Garry Shandling's Show, Bob, Frasier, NewsRadio, The Adventures of Brisco County, Jr., Just Shoot Me!, Now and Again, Nancy Kerrigan Special: Dreams on Ice, Dame Edna's Hollywood, The Unpleasant World of Penn & Teller, The Other Half, Jerry Lewis MDA Labor Day Telethon, Beverly Hills, 90210, Christmas in Rockefeller Center, Tom and Jerry, Deal or No Deal, Eli Stone, Ugly Betty, Lost, Undercovers*, and more. He has also provided the themes and underscore for *House of Mouse, The Marshall*, and *Our House*.

Dresel co-wrote *Gordon Goodwin's Big Phat Band Play-Along Series for Drums, Volume 1*. He holds a double Bachelor of Music in Percussion Performance and Music Education from the Eastman School of Music, and he currently teaches at the University of Nevada Las Vegas (UNLV) from Los Angeles.

THAT'S HOW WE ROLL
Performance Notes

By Gordon Goodwin

When I wrote this chart, it occurred to me that it summed up the vibe of our band pretty well. It had a hip, forward-moving groove, a bluesy chord structure, and a hooky melody, sprinkled with more complex compositional content. It seemed just like us, which is why I named it "That's How We Roll."

The shuffle groove has always been a favorite of mine, and Bernie Dresel is a master at playing it. On this tune, the groove is a tight, more pop-oriented shuffle, and you will need to balance playing the shuffle snare pattern with catching some of the horn figures (for example, in mm. 19–20). In these measures, and when it recurs elsewhere in the chart, Bernie hits those offbeats right with the horns.

A particular request I make of the rhythm section: Be able to play at a softer volume at times without diminishing the intensity of the groove. The dynamic marking at m. 50 is *mf*, specifically, an assertive *mf*. It's not loud, exactly, but it needs to be strong while leaving room to go to another dynamic level when needed.

The solo section begins at m. 93, where you will accompany Eric Marienthal's exciting alto solo. Eric's solo is masterful; he shows how to sustain and build a solo over this long form, with increasing intensity, stunning technique, and an unswerving focus on groove and feel. Since the style of the groove leans toward pop, you will need to decide how much you should respond to Eric's solo and how much you should establish a nice rhythmic bed for him to play over. At the very least, you will want to shade your playing with dynamics during this section.

After the solo section, the band begins a long vamp that leads to a sax soli and then the shout chorus, which is set up by your exciting 2-bar solo fill in mm. 190–191. Remember that, in your attempt to create excitement here, you need to set up the trombones to come in correctly in m. 192, so be kind! Playing a ton of fancy notes may be exhilarating, but so is good musicality.

As for the shout chorus itself at m. 194—you can goose the band a little here, as you raise your game a notch and lead us to the end of the chart. Slam the stuffing out of those last four chords, and cue wild audience applause.

By Bernie Dresel

Set at about 180 BPM, "That's How We Roll" is a shuffle with a triplet groove. A swing feel can vary depending on tempo. Between 160 BPM and 240 BPM, it can morph from a triplet to a straight-eighth feel. I play shuffles in a variety of ways—using the right-hand ride to play the regular swing pattern, playing all the eighth notes with only the upbeats unaccented during slow-enough tempos, or even just playing quarter notes for extremely fast shuffles.

After having practiced quite a bit the last two years developing my left hand chops, I tend to now play all the eighth notes of a shuffle on the snare drum at all shuffle tempos. This is not necessary, but doing this can really propel the shuffle even more by having both the right hand on the ride and the left hand on the snare playing all the eighth notes. (*GG: He's right—we love it when he does that!*) It's almost like two drummers ganging up on the band and the groove. If you simply can't get either of these shuffle options for the snare drum, you at least should play the snare back beats with one preceding eighth note like this: 1 and 2, 3 and 4.

Catching the figures in a shuffle is very similar to catching them in a funk, Cuban, Brazilian, rock, or country two beat groove. These grooves have a very audible kick-and-snare pattern. To catch a figure, you will have to abandon the groove in one of the limbs or all of them. In a straight-ahead swing feel, the main groove involves the ride cymbal with a very soft backbeat hi-hat. The snare and kick drum are free to roam when you need them to catch a figure, but they are not essential to the groove. They may not play at all, or the bass drum would be "felt but not heard" on the quarter notes. So, they are essentially lying in wait to be available for figures. Even though the shuffle is practically in the swing family, the approach differs in that the kick and snare are very busy and involved in the basic beat. That means that when you play a figure within a shuffle context, you might play it with a kick drum, yet keep the snare and ride going. Playing a figure with the snare, you would maintain the kick, which might be a little louder than inaudible, and the ride. Another way to play the shuffle figure would be to catch a simple figure with an accented snare, but continue to play the other shuffling eighths around, albeit quieter.

Now, a backbeat can pull the style into the pop side of the swing groove. In this case, I chose to begin with the hi-hat on the full groove at m. 13; this implies a Chicago blues shuffle, which leans toward rock. Starting on the ride would have implied a more jazz-flavored shuffle.

Throughout mm. 19–20, you will have classic "drummy" offbeats to catch. Catch them all in the snare, right? Wrong! Our ears tell us the trombones are catching them. This means that you could catch these beats in the bass drum or use your left hand on the toms to play descending pitches that enhance the trombone line. You don't need eight toms to catch all the pitch changes—just a general "down the toms" over two measures will do the trick.

The goal on any chart is to voice the drum kit correctly for the band. In general, voice the trumpets on snare, the bones on toms or bass drum, short notes with the drums, and long notes using cymbals in the figure. But, if you hit a crash on a short note or a snare on a bone hit, it won't sound like a huge mistake. You win some; you lose some. You just want to get a high batting average. The band will sound tighter, and you will sound better!

Look for the opportunity to get off the hi-hat and onto the ride. Play the solos at mm. 93–140 and the shout chorus at mm. 194–208—the peak of excitement! Go get 'em, tiger!

THAT'S HOW WE ROLL

Drums

By Gordon Goodwin (ASCAP)

That's How We Roll

THAT'S HOW WE ROLL

That's How We Roll

RIPPIN 'N RUNNIN'
Performance Notes

By Gordon Goodwin

Funk music is the best! I love playing and writing it. In "Rippin 'n Runnin," I decided to make some embellishments—you'll notice that this tune can get a little dissonant at times and the groove has details to it. You aren't just plowing away at the funk groove; there are figures the rhythm section has to play, as in mm. 38–42. It's not that those four measures are that hard to execute; it's more about transitioning from the more "groovy" parts to the more specific parts. Really, every note in the chart should sound like you are playing it by ear, not reading written-out music. While you could make the case that this is a worthy goal for every chart you play, it seems especially crucial for this kind of music, which is so reliant on intuition and feel. That feel must remain in place at all times. Throughout written parts, the solo section, fills…everywhere! I suppose I could ask that of every single band member, but a horn player can get away with dropping the feel for a minute. But the drummer? Cue that car-crash sound effect!

The solo section starts at m. 108. You will enjoy playing behind three world-class alto saxophonists, Gerald Albright, Dave Koz, and Eric Marienthal. Stay aware of which guy is playing at a given time, and see how each soloist affects your choices.

After the solos, the development section begins at m. 176, and the dynamic level comes down to *mf*. We still need forward propulsion, but it needs to be soft enough so that you can hear all those cool horn lines . . . I know they're cool, 'cause Wayne Bergeron told me so. The band eventually begins cookin' again. By m. 228, we are charging to the end of the chart. And your fill in m. 250? You know what to do—*take no prisoners, baby!*

By Bernie Dresel

In "Rippin 'n Runnin'," I chose to play a different groove than what is on the page. Searching for a groove that may be better than the one written is always the drummer's and the band leader's prerogative. When we rehearsed it for the first time, playing the snare on beats 2 and 4 gave the groove an almost pedestrian rock sound. I chose to go with "four on the floor": quarter notes on the bass drum with a half-time reggae feel in my hands. This seemed to do the trick and make Gordon smile. (*GG: I'm usually a happy guy.*)

I also chose to start the half-time backbeat at m. 1 with a side stick rather than snare. The chart does not say to do that, but I was looking for a way to build by adding the snare later. It is also a reggae thing to do. But at m. 108, I thought what Gordon wrote to play was perfect in its uniqueness. Without the bass playing, it seems like a groovy ticking clock. So I honored his part through the solo sections.

Playing reggae with four on the floor opens you up to fills or "events" in the vein of Stewart Copeland (drummer for The Police). Look for spaces such as mm. 98–100 to throw these events in. But be careful, as you are not the only rhythm-section player who wants to add fills. Try not to play on top of other rhythm players' events, and they will hopefully be just as considerate. In general, play well with others. Wait . . . isn't that a Wayne Bergeron album title?

Again, we find the figure with caps to catch in m. 42, m. 97, m. 223, m. 231, and the last measure, m. 251. This reoccurring rhythmic theme sounds and looks like an obvious "catch" to play. Since we are in a quirky reggae feel, I chose to catch it not just in the snare this time, but as a pseudo-timbale sound with a rim shot. This involves playing the rim and head at the same time, with one stick on a tom, or a rim shot snare, or, even quirkier, with a rim shot on a snare as I muffle it with my other hand. And for the sake of the groove, play these five eighth notes in a row all with the right hand: RRRRR (do not alternate: LRLRL). This enables the right-hand eighth-note party you have in the hi-hat to continue on the eighth-note timbale fill.

Make sure to play the accents on the hi-hat that Gordon notated in mm. 64–71 and mm. 237–242. They are not just random accents, but, compositionally, important to the horns. To play these, I chose to keep constant eighths in my right hand while playing the accents with my left hand, creating "flat flams"—flams in which both hands play at the same time with no audible space between them. This will help the groove by having the right hand continuously play eighths. And you can see (and hear) that the specifically written, yet fun bass drums are low punches to catch.

At mm. 124–127 and mm. 140–143, the time is finally right to play the beat-2-and-4 snare lick that Gordon wrote in this chart. The next part of the solo section, at m. 144, needs a lift, as bass player Rick Shaw becomes more active. So for the first time, I go to the half-time snare with the four-on-the-floor kick drum returning. I introduce hi-hat offbeats and eventually build to ride-bell offbeats, while looking for moments to interject "events" with the all-star saxophone soloists! In this section, anything can happen differently from performance to performance, while maintaining a very similar shape and groove.

At m. 176, the feeling relaxes and settles after all the major activity has hopefully broken loose in the solo section. I chose to go with a more pedestrian-rock kick-drum beat, abandoning the propulsive bass-drum quarters, and bringing back the ticking-clock side stick from m. 108.

Measures 208–209 feature a 2-bar drum fill. Based on the material that surrounds those measures, this shouldn't be treated as a spotlight moment; a quirky fill works well here, so I displaced the downbeats to achieve this.

Some of the drum fills in this chart seem like they could have a "pop mentality" of duplication. I made the solo fill at mm. 41–42 part of the composition by playing it exactly the same at mm. 96–97. You could, however, vary it for the final fill at m. 250. This fill puts the tune to bed with an exciting "look what I can do mom" flourish.

Now . . . let 'er rip!

RIPPIN 'N RUNNIN'

Drums

By Gordon Goodwin (ASCAP)

RIPPIN 'N RUNNIN'

WHY WE CAN'T HAVE NICE THINGS
Performance Notes

By Gordon Goodwin

"Why We Can't Have Nice Things" is a flag-waving, barn-burning, straight-ahead swing chart, in which you, the drummer, get all the big bucks! This is big band heaven, baby, so jump in and start kickin' it!

As in most of my big band drum parts, you will see horn cues above the staff. I'm not implying that you should catch or accent every one of those figures. Your experience, taste, and judgment will play a large part in deciding what is appropriate to catch and what is not. Trust that I'll write out any figure that I definitely want played, as in m. 8 or mm. 51–52. On the other hand, m. 17, m. 18, and m. 19 have informational horn cues that don't need to be played unless you want to. As you learn the lay of the land of this arrangement, you can refine your choices and priorities.

You are swinging along through the entire six-and-half-minute chart, so find places to enhance the colors in the arrangement by playing different dynamic levels, ride cymbals, patterns, etc. You will have more latitude for this kind of expression in the solo section at m. 110. Listen closely to Kevin Garren's alto solo and Andy Martin's trombone solo, and adjust accordingly. Play *with* those guys! Of course, in the real world, the soloists would also respond to what you are playing, and the music would evolve further. For now, though, the communication can only go one way. Even so, those guys are burning it up, and it's really fun to play along with them.

In a chart like this, you will, as usual, lock in with the bass player (in this case, the Big Phat Band's bassist, Rick Shaw). Your right hand and Rick's right forefinger should be the best of musical friends. Equally important: Listen closely to the lead trumpet (the great Wayne Bergeron on this recording), who is determining the placement and interpretation of all the horn figures. For a chart like this, you three guys have the biggest impact on the pulse, the energy, and the flow. And when it's right, this kind of fast-paced tune can be one of the most exciting things in jazz. So . . . make it right!

By Bernie Dresel

In many swing charts, the bass drum doubles the upright or electric bass. In m. 1 of "Why We Can't Have Nice Things," the bass drum grabs the first two hits with the bass. In this case, it should be heard and played with a kind of dotted-quarter to eighth figure. When the bass starts walking at m. 17, suddenly drop that bass drum down to an inaudible range. This provides a little weight to the quarter-note bass figure and unifies the bass and drums. Without the bass drum playing, you would only hear the high-end parts of the drumset for the basic swing groove—ride cymbal, hi-hat, and maybe some snare. You can raise the volume at mm. 21–24, and lower it at m. 25.

But why should we play the bass drum at all if nobody's going to hear it? Well, it's felt and sympathetically heard. If the bass player did not play we would hear the bass drum, but it should be at such a low volume that the upright bass will cover it up. The tempo on this chart is 250 BPM. Play straight eighths

on the ride to set up figures and your solos, except when you play any triplets on your set-ups, fills, or solos.

Measures 73–78 will involve playing the ride pattern, which includes the bass drum (a little louder than before), and an open foot-pedal hi-hat on the backbeats of 2 and 4. You can still catch some of the ride on top with your left hand as your right hand helps play the figure on the snare. For example, catch beat 1 of m. 73, beat 4 of m. 73, and beat 3 of m. 74, and then repeat this at mm. 77–78. Basically, this implies some 3/4 horn phrasing over the 4/4 bass phrase—a very jazzy thing to do. And you get this section again at mm. 224–229. A word about the hi-hat foot in the swing feel: Don't stomp on it so loud that it starts to dominate in the drum mix. It shouldn't be that loud. Don't open it so far, and learn to play the hi-hat with your foot at different dynamic levels, or at least two dynamics, soft and loud. It shouldn't be a sound that is one volume all the time. When you get soft on the ride and the drum kit, make sure you are getting soft with your hi-hat foot as well. Practice making your ride cymbal feel strong and steady so that you don't rely on the hi-hat as a crutch of solidity while your ride is weak and messy.

Measure 178 exemplifies the type of artistic license that a drummer can bring to the table. It provides a written hi-hat part, but I decided to bring my rockabilly Brian-Setzer experience into the picture and play this section on the rim of the snare drum. If the leader doesn't like it, he'll tell you. You will, won't you, Gordon? (*GG: I have no idea what he's talking about.*) By starting this way, it gives me an opportunity to grow from practically nothing and build this section with the additive horn orchestration by adding hi-hat, snare, bass drum, cymbal, and more.

For the final hit on beat 2 of m. 250, you don't just want to hit a crash and a bass drum. We do that all the time when the horns hit a long ensemble note. They play a long fall and, therefore, you must, too. Hit the crash and bass drum to get it started, and then fall off with a buzz roll from loud to soft on the snare or toms. Again, try to copy the sound of the horns and the rest of the band with the drum kit as best you can. And never stop trying to improve or add to your arsenal of skills and be the best musician you can be. Try not to be discouraged by looking at things you need to improve on. Recognizing them is half the battle, but only half. The other half is simply *practice*!

WHY WE CAN'T HAVE NICE THINGS

By Gordon Goodwin (ASCAP)

Drums

GARAJE GATO
Performance Notes

By Gordon Goodwin

OK, don't think I didn't see your eyes light up when you saw this chart—m. 2 is marked with "Solo." The challenge is that it's an open solo. When playing this chart live, the band hits are on cue, but we couldn't really figure out a way for to make that happen on the TnT 2 software. The technology just isn't ready yet! So, I hope you'll settle for listening to the great Bernie Dresel and Joey De Leon battle it out at the beginning. You'll get your chance to solo later on in the chart, I promise.

Latin music is such a big part of the Big Phat Band repertoire. Each sub-genre that falls under the umbrella of "Latin music" has its own set of stylistic parameters, and we try to adhere to these rules, while attempting to stay artistically honest to ourselves. I love the fire and rhythmic emphasis of this style, as well as the harmonic and melodic richness. All of these factors come into play with "Garaje Gato," a tune named after our 20-year-old cat who loves spending time in our garage! Don't ask me why—a cat does what it wants, right?

Bernie will certainly get deep into some of the specific considerations in playing this kind of music, but let me deal with a few broad strokes.

On a tune like this, laying down the groove is your primary job. Since this is a big band chart, you may have more horn figures to catch than your typical Latin drummer. But as you catch those figures, the groove continues. It should continue throughout the melody section, the solo section, every transition, every written figure, and every figure you make up on your own. The groove should continue when you take a break to answer the phone and when you go to the kitchen to get something to eat. Do you get the point? The groove should never stop! Even when you are playing mm. 121–122, keep the rhythmic pulse in your body. This will make it much easier for the rest of the band to lock in on the time; they know that you are committed to the groove, that you are rock solid, and that they can always rely on you to show everybody where things are.

Having said that, we don't want a drum machine. (It cracks me up that the term "drum machine" has become an antiquated term. Perhaps I should have said, "We don't want a 100-percent-quantized drum loop.") There are circumstances in which the time needs to bend a little. The trick is to allow that to happen in an organic way. For instance, in m. 131, the Big Phat Band horn section chose to lay back a little on that lick. Stay alert for those moments, so that you can accommodate them when they happen. Sometimes this involves a conversation with the lead trumpet player or band director in advance, and sometimes it happens spontaneously.

When playing live, you will want to have a conversation with your percussionist, especially on a tune like this. As you play along, listen closely to all the great parts laid down by Big Phat Band percussionist Joey De Leon. Joey and Bernie worked closely together to decide who would do what on this chart, and that communication continued as they played together.

Your big drum solo begins at m. 184, where you trade with Joey.

Here's the plan: Joey for eight bars; you for eight bars; Joey for four bars; you for four bars; Joey for four bars; you for four bars; Joey for two bars; you for two bars; Joey for two bars; you for two bars; Joey for two bars; you for two bars; and Joey for two bars. Whew!

Of course, as the vamp builds and the trading breaks down, Joey and Bernie (you) can start playing at the same time.

I love hearing drummers solo over a pattern like this—dig in and have fun! And the next time I see the Garaje Gato, I'll give her your best.

By Bernie Dresel

"Garaje Gato" is a salsa tune with a 2-3 clave pattern. At this tempo, a half note equals 108 BPM. I play a *mambo* beat or its fraternal twin, the *songo* beat. We can call this a Latin tune, but it is not from the country of Latinia, although Gordon's cat may very well be from there. This chart has a Cuban feel, quite different from the Brazilian sound that typically categorizes Latin music. It is also not a bebop kitchen-sink Latin tune à la Art Blakey; this sound would combine a Brazilian bass drum with a psuedo-Cuban ride-bell pattern. The main drum groove's bass rhythm makes it much more specific and authentic to Cuba. And unlike most mambo or songo grooves, this one contains written-out notation. Note the bass drum part for the main groove is a typical Cuban bass rhythm. A lot of times there may be just the word mambo, songo, or salsa (or any other style groove) written at the beginning of the chart and no specific beat written, only slashes. It would then be up to you to know what that beat or some variation would be.

In this chart, there are actual notations of hi-hat and kick drum, etc., written out. You can decide to honor that and play exactly what's there, but many times the drummer will play something very similar that may be a little more "drummer-friendly" than what a composer may have chosen to write for you. It is up to you to decide what will sound best—this is usually the case about anything you decide to play. The audience, and often even the band leader, does not know what is exactly on the page (GG: *That's what you think, buddy . . .*), and most composers would agree that the drum part is just a strong "suggestion." They want you to "make it better" and play what will sound good. I sometimes refer to the horn players as the "readers," meaning actual exact rhythms and pitches are written for them to read and play unless there is an improv section. The drum part is very different in that it is just a guide that helps you see what others in the band are playing. You learn to do this by listening and watching recorded and live music in different genres and differently sized ensembles. There is so much to learn by doing this, which you cannot get from books or teachers telling you what to do! (GG: *Preach it, baby!*)

Measures 116–119 are an excellent example of what I call gear-shifting; the rhythm changes every few beats. In this case, it occurs every four. Generally, this concept should be practiced at different tempos and with different beat counts, backwards and forwards. You can also vary the techique by shifting between gears at different times, skipping a gear, changing the drum it's played on, etc. Once you're comfortable, you can use gear-shifting as a valuable tool in your soloing.

The soloing in this chart involves trading 8s and 4s and 2s with your percussionist. Ultimately, you should establish some original ideas in your solo as well as draw from the percussionist's solos. And you should use a Cuban-style vocabulary, derived from listening to, transcribing, and learning from various bongo, conga, and timbale players' solos. You don't have to play a transcribed solo note for note, but playing something conceptually similar to a transcribed-solo idea will still be in the spirit of jazz. Try to play specific rhythms and stickings, and not just what happens to come out when you move your hands around the kit.

GARAJE GATO

Drums

By Gordon Goodwin (ASCAP)

Garaje Gato

Garaje Gato

Garaje Gato

GAINING ON YOU
Performance Notes

By Gordon Goodwin

I hardly know what's gotten into me nowadays—what's with all the drum solos?

But, dude, you are going to have some fun on this one. Right off the bat, you get a 2-bar solo leading into an exclamatory six-note phrase that is, essentially, the structural pillar of this chart. No matter what fancy licks are going down, we eventually come back to these six notes, like a touchstone. During the intro, you are playing time, catching the horn figures, and soloing every two bars or so. We are just getting started!

The sax melody in m. 49 is fairly note-heavy, and during this section—actually, for much of this track—Bernie plays a quarter-note ride pattern, with accent variations and an occasional eighth note thrown in. He will no doubt elaborate on this topic, but to my ears, at this rapid tempo, a quarter-note ride-cymbal pattern sounds clean.

Listen to the complete version of our track, and check out what Bernie does on the ride cymbal during the beginning of my piano solo, around the 2-minute, 50-second mark. This is a great example of the many variations that can help change color and feel.

The solo section begins at m. 133 with two choruses featuring Brian Scanlon on tenor and two more featuring me on piano. Make us sound good.

After the solos, the development section pulls together our building-block lick, along with several other compositional fragments. Your time and soloing, in turn, hold the section together. Addressing all of these details can be tricky; it's similar to how you played during the intro, only more intense.

We eventually return to the melody at m. 209, as the chart begins revving up. Pay attention to beat 2 of m. 228. It's easy to miss accenting that second beat at this tempo, but it's important to hit this chord together and hit it strong. This chord helps transition into the final shout chorus at m. 229.

Once we get to the final Emi7 vamp at m. 245, you'll get to revisit a bunch of licks that have already appeared in the chart. I chopped the last two notes of the primary lick off the last two measures when I wrote the chart, though—I just couldn't bring myself to go, "DAT DAT DAT, DAH–Da DAT" one more time. Do I have to tell you to hit those last four chords as hard as you can? Nah, didn't think so.

By Bernie Dresel

All figures are not created equal. It is very important to voice your part to match the articulations and sound of the horns. For example, short notes in the horns should be short notes on a drum, and long notes in the horns should be long notes, played by using sustaining cymbals in addition to a drum. High notes in the horns (trumpets) could be your (high) snare drum. Low notes in the horns (bones and bari sax) could be your (low) toms or bass drum.

When you see a specific figure above slashes in the staff, as in mm. 3–4 or mm. 11–12 of "Gaining on You," play them on the snare drum with the left hand, and continue to play the ride cymbal with your right hand. Most times, when the band has caps, as written in these examples, there are trumpets or even all horns involved. This is a classic example of how you can match the sound of the trumpets, high and *staccato*, with the sound of the snare drum, high and *staccato*. A match made in drumset-voicing heaven!

Are the figures at mm. 23–24, mm. 85–86, mm. 167–168, and mm. 249–250 trumpets again? Not entirely. They are mostly saxes and unnecessary to catch. Or you could lightly shade them with a figure that includes light toms, a light shank on the ride with light bass drum, and a light snare buzz. And then, perhaps, finish the figure by playing the last one or two beats. And, as mentioned earlier, be careful with the articulations on these last two quarter notes. Beat 3 is long and could be a snare buzz or a ride-shank crash. In contrast, beat 4, marked *staccato*, could be a short snare or tom hit, as the high trumpets do not play here. But how do we know it is saxes there in this case? The chart does not always tell us who is playing these figures, so most of the time you have to use your ears to hear who is playing the figure and your eyes to by looking over your music stand at the horns to see who is getting ready to play the figure. This is why I like to set up with the horns on my hi-hat side. I put my music stand over the hi-hat enabling me to turn pages with my left hand and to see who is lifting their horn to their mouth. And if you have played the chart more than once, your memory or penciling it in the chart helps you remember who is going to play an upcoming figure. I've seen so many drummers read a chart and catch saxophone figures like they are brass figures, loud and percussive. But they are for a reed instrument and a completely different approach. Shade the saxes, don't catch them. (*GG: We saxes thank you . . .*) We should be able to listen to only the drum track and be able to tell what the horns are doing meaning articulations and which instruments are playing from the drum orchestration you choose to play.

Measures 91–92 are a classic example of short trombone figures. Play these figures on the toms, or the toms and bass drum, rather than the snare. Maybe even follow the contour of their pitch jump on the tom—high-high-low-high-high—or toms and bass drum—tom-tom-kick-tom-tom. And then, by hitting the short snare, play a final *staccato* hit on beat 4 with the trumpets and saxes. The rhythm is in the drum chart, but the instruments are not specified. Look at what Gordon wrote on mm. 265–266. They look the same as mm. 91–92, but I won't tell you what's different! Use your ears to decide what you need to do differently this time. Just reading the chart is not enough!

Instead of playing the entire figure in m. 95 with your left hand on the snare, you can stick that whole measure RLRLRLRL. Bail on playing the ride cymbal for that first beat, and bring the right hand down to the snare. Nobody will miss the ride cymbal for one beat—it's okay. Then, for beat 2, get right back up to the ride with your right hand. Pretty simple, and it flows!

For mm. 229–230 and mm. 237–238, you could keep the right hand on the ride, and play the figure with your left hand. Or, you could bail on the ride cymbal totally, and stick those two measures with RRRR, RRLLR. Crazy! That sticking gets you downbeats with your R and upbeats with your L. It grooves, and by bailing on the sustaining ride, you emphasize all the *staccato* notes even more.

And keep in mind, you can reference my notes about the fast swing feel in "Race to the Bridge" for this tune.

GAINING ON YOU

Drums

By Gordon Goodwin (ASCAP)

IT'S NOT POLITE TO POINT
Performance Notes

By Gordon Goodwin

What model citizens most trombone players are. They sit there, in the middle of the band, holding things together like an offensive line on a football team. Cue the trumpets and saxes with their "They're offensive, all right!" jokes, as the saxes and trumpets get all the features and all the glory. Well, I had just enough of that injustice, so I wrote this chart to try and set things straight. The funny thing was, after we recorded this, I wasn't 100-percent sure that it would make the record. But people kept saying things like, "Whatever you do, don't cut that trombone song." And now, when we play it live, it's a high point for our set. Shows what I know, I guess.

Your job here is pretty straight-ahead—get this chart swingin'! The solo section begins at m. 79. Measure 123 starts an extended trombone soli; you can choose which figures to catch. Bernie will have cogent advice in that respect, but this section is a bit unique in that the bass player is not playing a walking bass line. Instead, he is playing the same figures as the trombones. The guitar is playing Freddie-Green-style quarter-note strums. (Freddie Green was the guitar player for Count Basie's band for like, 50 years. No kidding—he did it for 50 years!) You and the Big Phat Band guitar player Andrew Synowiec (Freddie Green had a low E string that was older than Andrew!) and are the primary time keepers in this section. This trombone soli gradually builds to, in all modesty, one of my favorite moments in this chart. Sometimes, the composing comes easily for me, and sometimes, it's hard. The shout chorus at m. 167 came out quickly, easily, and naturally. It has a nice flow to it, and I love watching and listening to Bernie Dresel kick its daylights out. Bernie raises his game even more at the modulation at m. 191. You should do that, too!

The chart is now over, so congratulate the trombones for doing a great job on a difficult piece of music. And then, you should immediately go back to making trombone jokes. Hey, I don't make the rules, folks.

By Bernie Dresel

Now, as you probably know, in general, trombone players are very nice people—relaxed and maybe a little late to the party at times (GG: Whoa, harsh, dude!). They also didn't pick to play the highest brass instrument, the trumpet. Consequently, they may occasionally be a little behind the beat. It is very important on this trombone feature not to let the 115-BPM tempo go in the toilet. Even though the reoccurring dotted-quarter-to-eighth-note push is in the whole rhythm section and bones, you should feel the intensity of the quarter-note pulse in your head. If you keep landing on the "and" of beat 2, the pulse can start to slow down. So, I will catch this "and" of beat 2 in the bass drum, snare, or tom, but not always with the ride cymbal. Sometimes, I plow ahead and hit beat 3, just to keep the time honest. Especially at the beginning of this tune, when the band is *mp* and not in a "4" feel, it is important to establish the tempo and avoid letting it immediately sink.

As I play the ride-cymbal swing feel at 115 BPM, the rhythm feels triplet-based. In a large ensemble with 13 horns, a strong, accented quarter-note feel is important at any tempo slower than 160 BPM. Listen to all the Count Basie drummers, Buddy Rich, Mel Lewis, myself on this chart, and even Jimmy Cobb on the small-group Miles Davis record *Kind of Blue*, play this quarter-note accent in the ride cymbal: DANG-DANG-ga-DANG-DANG-ga-DANG. We play the ride on all four quarter notes in a measure, rather than just beats 2 and 4, which are also played on the hi-hat. It is important to make sure the unaccented notes, the "and" of beat 2 and the "and" of beat 4, remain soft and close to the cymbal. The pattern will enhance the bass player's groove, BOOM-BOOM-BOOM-BOOM (rather than boom-BOOM-boom-BOOM), when he finally goes into "4" at m. 15. When the bass player is in a "2" feel you could still create energy

by doing the quarter accents, or in the case of measure 1, you could do accents on beats 1, 2, the "and" of 2, and 4. The "little" notes would be the "and" of 3 and the "and" of 4. You want that energy, not lethargic, uninspired strokes on the cymbal. Dig in at any volume and any feel. Practice this tempo with a metronome with and without your bass player, so you can feel like you've been here before. It's a notch on your belt that you go to and stay at this tempo even if the band is "laying back."

Dynamic shaping helps sell Gordon's great charts. This one starts at *mp*. To begin, I use my alternate ride, my darker jazz ride, or my crash, and save the main ride, which is pingier, brighter, and more articulate, for the louder *tutti* ensemble stuff later. I considered starting with the hi-hat, but it just didn't seem right. Consider various ways to play parts, and then pick what you think is the best choice. What should be hit on the "and" of beat 4 of m. 40? Using your ears, notice that the sound includes very high, bell-like piano, guitar, and four harmon trumpets. How about playing a cymbal or cymbal bell? Yes, that would sound the most like that instrumentation.

At m. 43, I give the part a little more gas by playing *mf*. For the trumpet's *staccato*, off-beat eighth note on the "and" of beat 3, use a biting snare drum hit to maintain that dynamic level. As several figures are occurring, decide what to catch, what to leave out, and what to catch it with. Again, you should practice this chart one *measure* at a time, as well as one *section* at a time, and listen to the track without playing just to hear what is being played. You can loop desired sections or measures with the TNT 2 software—very cool.

For a younger or less-experienced big band drummer, the chart can initially be a lot to digest. But eventually, you will be able to hear what's going on as you play. And you will use your memory more than the chart itself to realize what to play and what is coming. And that brings up an important point: it's important to get your head "out of the chart" as much as possible. You will play with more authority if you can look at the ride cymbal, drum, or crash cymbal that you are striking. This also helps you to sell your performance to the audience. And it enables you to look at the band and hear even more. Did you ever see Led Zeppelin using music stands? (*GG: Did you ever see Led Zeppelin do anything?*)

Measures 66–67 is an interesting yet challenging transitional moment. You are at *f* for the first time in this chart, but the trumpets do not enter until the second half of the measure. Therefore, you need more gas for the *crescendo* into the downbeat of m. 67. Even though the ensemble is at full volume here, it's a little leap of faith that you have to lead the band, not react to them later.

Measure 79 at the solo section has a tight feel that harks a little to a '20s or '30s vaudeville-style, *staccato* quarter-note feel—therefore, *not* a swinging quarter-note ride.

Measure 167 is our climactic, swinging-backbeat shout chorus! Though the drum chart does not indicate playing a backbeat here, I decided that it would be appropriate and the most exciting choice. I based this on similar big band charts with a big, shuffling kick line. There is not always one best choice, but you want to pick what you think is in everything you play, and go with that.

And as far as the title of this tune goes, always remember, it is not only OK to be different socially, musically, personally, and so on, it is applauded and welcomed at the end of the day. This is probably why people remark to Gordon, "You have to have this trombone feature on the record." In a sea of saxophone, trumpet, and drum features, this chart sticks out as a must-have. Let that be a lesson to all of us on the greatness of uniqueness. Now, that being said, when we are musically collecting vocabulary, we initially copy others—hopefully, a multitude of others. But the challenge and the path to greatness is to then find a way to twist and mix up all the different approaches, and make them your own. People will "point" to you and say that your uniqueness is great, and it will be in a very "polite" way: "I love you!"

IT'S NOT POLITE TO POINT

By Gordon Goodwin (ASCAP)

Drums

It's Not Polite to Point

IT'S NOT POLITE TO POINT

It's Not Polite to Point

HOWDIZ SONGO?
Performance Notes

By Gordon Goodwin

Welcome to the chart with the worst pun and, therefore, the best title ever!

A *songo* groove basically means an Afro-Cuban feel. There are strong elements of it in this chart, along with other influences.

I am going to defer to Bernie Dresel about specific stylistic guidelines. On a chart like this, he's going to know better than me. My drum notation will usually be pretty close, and I will definitely be accurate about displaying what the horn section is doing. But when it comes to notation of the groove itself, listening to my man Bernie may be the best choice.

You're going to be plenty busy on this chart. By laying down the groove, setting up the horn licks, and interacting with your percussionist, you're going to have some serious fun.

The solo section begins at m. 68. If desired, you can change the feel. You'll no doubt want to take some inspiration from the soloists, Andrew Synowiec on guitar and Wayne Bergeron on the trumpet. Maybe, when Wayne starts playing high notes, you can switch to brushes . . . just kidding.

After the solos, the pianist plays a fun *montuno* figure that sets up a long, intensifying vamp, and boy, does he nail it! (Who is that guy, anyway?) The horns come in little by little and layer countermelodies over the groove. (Boy, is that piano player nailing it!) Meanwhile, you are playing time, catching the horn licks, and helping to build the intensity of the vamp. Things finally come together in m. 138 with three big *tutti* chords. You have a few measures to play your coolest, slickest fill, until the modulation and shout chorus and then the end of the chart.

This kind of music demands your commitment and passion. The entire band keys off the energy you bring to this tune. If you mess something up because you were really going for it, you won't hear me complaining. This chart includes several details to address, but once those are set, you should greatly enjoy playing this style . . . not to mention, playing along with that amazing piano player. Anybody have his email? I gotta drop that guy a note.

By Bernie Dresel

Gordon mentions the energy that you must bring to this tune. No matter how advanced you are as a drummer, energy is the one element you always need to bring to the table. It is also the one thing that you can emulate from your favorite drummers, even if you don't have some of their technical skills yet, and that the audience feels and remembers the most! It is important to groove and have things feel good—this is surely way up at the top of the list. But if the music feels lethargic, uninspired, or dynamically monotonous, your audience will be bored no matter how much it's groovin'.

So, how do we get that energy? It starts in the brain with an attitude. If you don't feel it there, it won't happen. You might even have to pretend that you're diggin' in and creating an intensity that doesn't naturally come for you. But no matter how hard you think about being energetic, something has to fire physically to manifest into a felt and perceived energy. Usually more easily created when playing at high volumes or with more aggression, energy is difficult to create when playing at lower volumes. Use the fingers to create accents and energy. You don't need to maintain "white-knuckle" tension in the hands, but you should hit the drum or cymbal with a spike-and-release technique—your fingers will resemble the line on a heart monitor. To play the *songo* feel of this chart, you would accent the quarter notes with your right hand, simulating the Cuban quarter-note bongo bell. (*GG: Or a Will Ferrell-style, quarter-note cowbell feel, for you* SNL *fans.*)

Again, you want to shape this chart with peaks and valleys, as if you and your listening audience are journeying somewhere. Listen to the great big band drummers, and take note of how they shape a chart. Where is the peak of the chart? Usually, it is during a shout chorus in the last third or fourth section. Aim for this moment. There may be other peaks, like the intro, the "send-off" into the first solo, or the end of a solo.

This tune has a *songo* feel with a 2-3 clave. *Songo* is the fraternal twin of the fast *mambo*. Mambo was historically played without drumset. The traditional Cuban percussion section involved timbales with cha cha and mambo cowbells, congas, bongos, and, occasionally, a bongo bell, which was more quarter-note based. As Cuba progressed and added the drumset, the section developed into a drumset with cowbells and congas and bongos played by one percussionist.

To play a mambo on the drumset, you would use busy, authentic mambo patterns. However, the songo usually involves more quarter-note-based bell patterns on the drumset's hi-hat, ride cymbal, or cowbell, and at the same time, incorporates funk, soul, and all other drumset elements. The songo bass patterns and the kick drum patterns may have more downbeats on beat 1 in the groove than a mambo pattern. The accented quarter-note bell part is filled in with extra unaccented sixteenth notes, which are written for the hi-hat in m. 1. You likely won't see the accents written on the quarter notes, but you should play them in this groove. As Gordon says, when you get to the solo section, you could "open it up" a little more, and you and your bass player may decide to include more elements of the traditional mambo, if desired.

Remember, charts are just a guide, written in this case by an amazingly great piano player and writer, not a drummer. Make music! Nobody who may be listening gets a copy of your chart and sees what's written; they only hear what you play. Make it an energetic, great journey!

HOWDIZ SONGO?

Drums

By Gordon Goodwin (ASCAP)

Howdiz Songo?

DOES THIS CHART MAKE ME LOOK PHAT?
Performance Notes

By Gordon Goodwin

When I compose, sometimes my goal will be to create something new and distinctive, something I haven't written before. And sometimes I want to, figuratively speaking, slip on a pair of old slippers. This is what I did with "Does This Chart Make Me Look Phat?" This chart is a straight-ahead, Count Basie-style arrangement, written in the arranging style of Sammy Nestico or Frank Foster. There were guidelines I followed to stay within the scope of this musical style, and you, the musician, will need to acknowledge similar rules when executing this music. The foremost of these may be time and feel. Generally speaking, young musicians have a more difficult time playing this kind of swing tune, for the simple reason that they haven't listened and internalized the style that much. There is no better way to grasp the nuance of swing music than to get your hands on a Count Basie record, and just listen to it—over and over. While it may initially sound somewhat dated, the more you listen, the more you will start to empathize with it. The music will start to reveal its secrets to you.

Bernie Dresel will speak to many of the technical considerations involved in playing this kind of swing chart, but I'd say that in a broad sense, this kind of chart requires more innate musicality from the drum chair than many other styles. You will need to whisper at times and kick butt at others, while maintaining the swing feel. Everyone in the band must swing at all times, but they get that groove from you. If you are swinging hard, it becomes so much easier for the entire band. Swing away, throughout every hit and every fill. Even if you don't catch a single horn-section accent, make sure to swing with every breath, beginning at m. 1, beat 1.

This stuff is exactly why many of us fell in love with big band jazz. Digging into a cool chart (if I may say so) and swinging hard as a unit—man, it's the best! It's so fun that when the chart ends, we count it off and play it again. This is what we do at m. 197, only up a half step!

Count Basie put his first band together in the 1930s, and today, almost 80 years later, the principles of large-ensemble swing that he helped organize are still with us and relevant—and that ain't bad.

By Bernie Dresel

When a chart gets put on your stand for the first time, you will want to look the "test" over before you are allowed to pick your pencil (sticks) up. You should not be looking at the chart for the first time as you play it for the first time. That being said, you probably only have a minute or two to look at it. So, you should always skim the chart over very quickly for any problem figures, especially figures that appear unfamiliar or complicated. Is there a D.C. or a D.S.? Where does the D.S. go back to? Is there a "to coda" spot and if so, where is the coda? What is the rhythm on the last bar of the piece? If it says Latin, you would want to know if it was a Cuban or Brazilian bass rhythm, for instance. In this case, it is swing, and you wonder, would it always be in a "4" feel, or always in "2"? Or does it switch back and forth, and if so, where? And of course, you will definitely use your ears on the fly to figure out what the bass is playing. Your ears are your most important tool, and they will fill in the missing info a chart and your eyes do not provide.

For the basic swing feel at this fast tempo, you will want that quarter-note accent on every downbeat to lock in with the bass. Play a straight up-and-down, accented quarter-note feel in the ride pattern or hi-hat pattern—lay it down! The feathered "felt-but-not-heard" bass drum should, however, follow the bass, whether it has a "4" or "2" feel.

And by all means, you and the bass player must be on the same page tempo-wise. Yes, you are a team, but you are the president, while the bass player is the vice president—that rule must follow you over the cliff, whether you are right or wrong. If the tempo slows down (or speeds up), you, the drummer, rather than the bass player, will be blamed or told to do a better job of holding a steady tempo. In this case, you drop out for seven measures at m. 46, and the bass player becomes the president during that time. However, if the tempo has decreased or increased by the time you re-enter with brushes at m. 53, it is your responsibility to return to the original tempo and avoid taking the new one—just maintain it for the last 160 measures! Any tempo "discussions" between you and the bass player, or with anyone else in the band, should always be diplomatic and loving, yet firm—you are the drummer, responsible for the tempo. (*GG: We love you, too, Bernie.*)

Skim the chart to look ahead for dynamic changes. Pay attention to places with a sudden *p* or a *ff* peak to aim for. This will give shape to the chart and make it musical and effective. Aiming for these highs and lows will help you *lead* the band, as well, just like a conductor feeding the ensemble dynamic direction. In this chart, there are no *pp* or *p* markings, only *mp*. So, it would be good to exaggerate the dynamics or widen them by making the *mp* actually *pp*. Audiences are usually bombarded by bands playing the same volume all the time. Instead, you can really capture the band's attention by occasionally playing very softly. When playing softly, keep your stick heights low. However, maintain the intensity in your hands and head as if you are digging in and playing loud. Brushes will naturally lower the volume (at m. 53, for example), but you will need to get way down from m. 1 until the surprise *sfz* at m. 25. Measure 78 will be the loudest moment of the piece until that point. And then, at m. 96, you will eclipse that volume even more. Each of those loud moments are brief; you'll usually be at a comfortable *mf*. At m. 144, exaggerate the *mp* down to *p* once again, and then that explosive *sfz* at m. 146 will be even more effective.

When you solo, remember to land at *mf* at m. 97. Here, the small group of players should be at a dynamically appropriate level—soft, for one solo instrument rather than 4–13 horns possibly playing at once!

Let's look at mm. 142–143. This figure would be a shuffle groove of offbeats in the snare, different from a shuffle groove with backbeats on the snare, if it were to be repeated continuously. Practice playing this figure by playing it over and over again. You will not only learn to play the correct rhythm but also how to groove and make the music feel good. "It don't mean a thing if it ain't got that swing!" So, feel applies to parts you only play once in a chart, not just the basic groove. Practice this constantly—groove and feel are everything!

DOES THIS CHART MAKE ME LOOK PHAT?

Drums

By Gordon Goodwin (ASCAP)

Slow greasy swing ♩ = 109

Does This Chart Make Me Look Phat?

Does This Chart Make Me Look Phat?

RACE TO THE BRIDGE
Performance Notes

By Gordon Goodwin

George Gerswhin's "I Got Rhythm" may be the most popular standard among jazz musicians. Not the melody, of course (we all pretty much ignore that), but those chord changes? That's meat and potatoes for us! "Race to the Bridge" is based on those famous changes, written to be a musical high-wire act that features each section of the band and many of our powerful soloists. On our live gigs, we play this chart at a "pretty damn fast" tempo, but for the recording, we settled on merely "really fast."

This chart is 380 bars long—more than that, actually, if you count the repeats in the solo section. That is a long span of time to play a fast swing pattern on the ride cymbal. Bernie will definitely have comments about this from an endurance point of view, but consider it from a musical point of view, as well. How can you vary your pattern and your sound so that this chart has contour? You may make different choices for each of the featured solis; the trombones at m. 41, the trumpets at m. 81, and the saxes at m. 121. Of course, to complicate the decision, you have three big 8-bar solos (starting at m. 73, m. 113, and m. 153); each one will make you want to release your inner Buddy Rich while adequately setting up the next section's entrance. Fact: You will learn that the band *always* appreciates a clear set-up for their entrance. If you nail the fanciest polyrhythms in your solo, but the band comes in at the wrong time, and it creates a big train wreck . . . well, it really can't be considered a successful solo, can it? We are all playing music *together*, and we should help each other play at the highest level possible. Bernie will bring his years of experience and valuable advice to this question. The good news: When it comes to this play-along, you can play almost anything on your solo, because these guys will come in at the same time, guaranteed! But with live music, always set up the band so that an entrance seems clear and logical.

The solo section begins at m. 201 with exciting solos by Eric Marienthal on alto sax and Brian Scanlon on tenor sax. Enjoy playing with those bad boys! After the solos, the development section starts at m. 265, where you have plenty of hits to catch and dynamics to play. Eventually, you drive the band home at m. 337, but not before another big moment for you: your solo at m. 353. It's "go-for-it" time, although you will need to incorporate the written figures that appear every two bars or so. No biggie, right?

This chart is definitely a bit of a workout. But like any good workout, you will feel invigorated afterwards. So go forth, unafraid, and dive straight in to "Race to the Bridge."

By Bernie Dresel

So, you want enough endurance to play fast on the ride cymbal for a very long time? Stay with low stick height on the cymbal, and make sure all notes hit the same spot. This will result in softer volume, less air space to travel, the stick not having to move as quickly through the air, and, therefore, the endurance you want. Stay relaxed. As soon as you tense up and start pushing and tightening muscles in your hand and forearm, the sooner you will get tired. You can also occasionally play quarter notes if you get tired or want some relief, but you must make it sound like this is being done for musical reasons.

In this chart, don't try to play the swing ride cymbal with a triplet-based feel. Any swing-ride cymbal pattern faster than 240 BPM should actually be straight eighths—that's right, straight eighths! The tempo for "Race to the Bridge" is usually set at 290 BPM (or faster, if Gordon wants us to sweat a little more). Hey, you'd think he was from the east coast! (*GG: We sweat in L.A., too!*) In addition, any triplet eighth notes can be played as triplets. At 290 BPM, these eighth-note triplets will be 870 strokes per minute; that's doable for most drummers, especially if RLL, RLL or RRL, RRL or RLL, and RRL (6-stroke roll), as well as RLR and LRL, stickings are incorporated. And any of those could be turned into inverse stickings, starting with L.

Trading begins to appear in the chart at m. 41. The trombones start with a 32-bar statement. The drums answer with an 8-bar solo break at m. 73. At m. 81, the trumpets have a 32-bar soli, which is followed by an 8-bar drum solo break at m. 113. Next, there's a 32-bar sax soli with two beats of sixteenth-note pickups, followed by a 6-bar drum break leading into two bars of low half notes. Wait . . . is that a fair trade: 32 vs. 8? OK, we'll take it! On any drum breaks or solos that are two bars or longer, be aware that the first part of the break is your solo. The very last part of the drum break is a set-up for the band—17 other guys, in this case—to feel comfortable with entrances. So, any 8-bar drum breaks should be considered as six bars of solo plus a 2-bar set-up. That set-up should be more straight up and down and on the beat than the solo. And it should be followed by a strong downbeat, in case the band has gotten lost. Also, playing the hi-hat on beats 2 and 4 throughout the eight bars, and maybe even adding the bass drum on all four beats, might not be a bad thing, if needed.

Your 8-bar solo drum breaks should incorporate some of the rhythms that Gordon has written for the horn soli. Measures 41–42 and mm. 45–46 have some nice *staccato* dotted quarters that start off the beat in the bones. Then, m. 47 has an eighth-quarter-eighth rhythm that you could pull from. Measures 65–66 and mm. 67–68 also include a nice rhythmic motif. You don't have to copy these rhythms exactly, but it's hip to keep them in mind and play off them. The 32-bar trumpet and sax solis contain many eighth-note runs rather than rhythmic statements and don't offer much material to play off. Remember, eight bars goes by very quickly at this tempo, so you don't have much time to develop something. In general, the breaks should be fast, exciting, "drummy" bursts of solo energy. Oh, yeah . . . and again, remember, do not "lose" the horns or slow down, and all the other stuff, too! You could practice getting your hand speed up to throw in the occasional sixteenth notes by using your fingers, not just wrists. Play RRRR, RRRR, RRRR, RRRR, LLLL, LLLL, LLLL, LLLL, using only your middle finger to move the stick, then only your ring finger, then only your pinky, and then all fingers with no wrist motion to build up hand speed. Continue to mark your progress day to day with a metronome to track your speed. Take breaks to rest when you get tired, so you don't start pushing and hurt yourself. Again, there is no substitute for practice time. Practice like that could even be done while you're watching the Dodgers play on television or Tony Williams play on YouTube.

RACE TO THE BRIDGE

Drums

By Gordon Goodwin (ASCAP)

Race to the Bridge

Race to the Bridge

RACE TO THE BRIDGE

TRANSCRIBED DRUM SOLOS
Performance Notes

By Gordon Goodwin

Congratulations! If you have gotten to this part of the book, you are now a master of big band ensemble playing. Well, maybe not a master, but I bet you've improved a lot. That's the good news. The bad news is that you are only half-finished. If your goal is to be a member of a group like the Big Phat Band, there's a little matter of improvisation to deal with. Becoming a proficient improviser is a lifelong pursuit. It's not just a matter of "playing what you feel," even though what you play must be an honest representation of your feelings.

But before we get to that part, you need to learn a basic vocabulary. You need to learn chords, scales, and how they fit together. There are plenty of books and other materials available for you to get that information, so we won't cover that here. Instead, this section of the book includes a few solo transcriptions for you to play and study. Examining transcriptions like these can be an important step in putting together your own style and method of improvising. The goal is not to regurgitate other people's licks and devices, even though there is no law against doing that. But learning other people's solos can provide a launching point for you to develop ideas.

We all have influences and musicians that we admire. They can exert a powerful pull on our musical aesthetic—don't resist this. Absorb the lessons from each musician, and continue to listen and search for other comparable musicians. Before you know it, you will have your own point of view and, most importantly, your own style.

The following page contains a few transcribed solos from featured players in the Big Phat Band. These solos are not on the play-along tracks on the disk. So, to hear these solos in context, you'll need to check out the Big Phat Band recordings with the solos.

Here are my recommendations for these transcribed solos (or any transcribed solos):

1. Listen to the original artist play the solo as you follow along with the music.

2. Slowly play through the solo by yourself, without the track and as an étude. Take your time examining how the solo is constructed; study the logic and the pacing of the solo, and pay attention to note choices and how they fit the harmony.

3. Play the solo with the track. After you can play it through, try to incorporate spontaneity. The real challenge with improvisation, then, becomes playing a spontaneous solo that maintains logic and structure.

At least, that's what I try to do. A balance in left- and right-brain thinking is a goal for me, not just in music, but in life as a whole. This process may or may not be the right approach for you.

If you are the type who likes to just jump in and see what happens by surviving on your wits, go for it! That's what's cool about a life in music—as you mature and discover things about your music, you also discover things about yourself.

The solos in this series were transcribed by Benny Golbin and Hal Rosenfeld, and they feature these talented members of the Big Phat Band:

- Wayne Bergeron (trumpet)
- Bernie Dresel (drums)
- Gordon Goodwin (tenor sax)
- Eric Marienthal (alto sax)
- Andy Martin (trombone)
- Brian Scanlon (tenor sax)

RACE TO THE BRIDGE

Bernie Dresel's Drum Solo Transcription

Drums Solo

By Gordon Goodwin (ASCAP)
Transcribed by Hal Rosenfeld

* When played at this tempo, this will sound like fragmented 8th notes. When slowed down, this is the clear rhythm.

GARAJE GATO
Bernie Dresel's Drum Solo Transcription

Drums Solo

By Gordon Goodwin (ASCAP)
Transcribed by Hal Rosenfeld

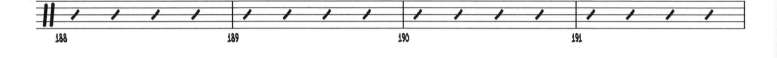

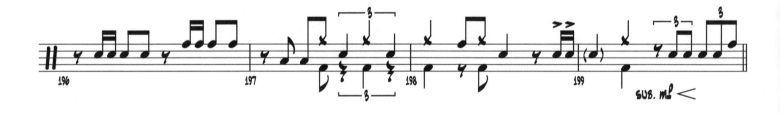

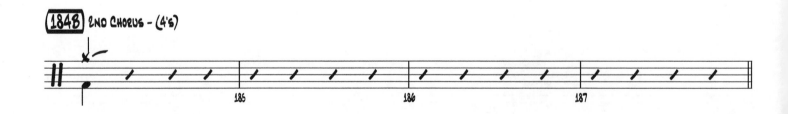

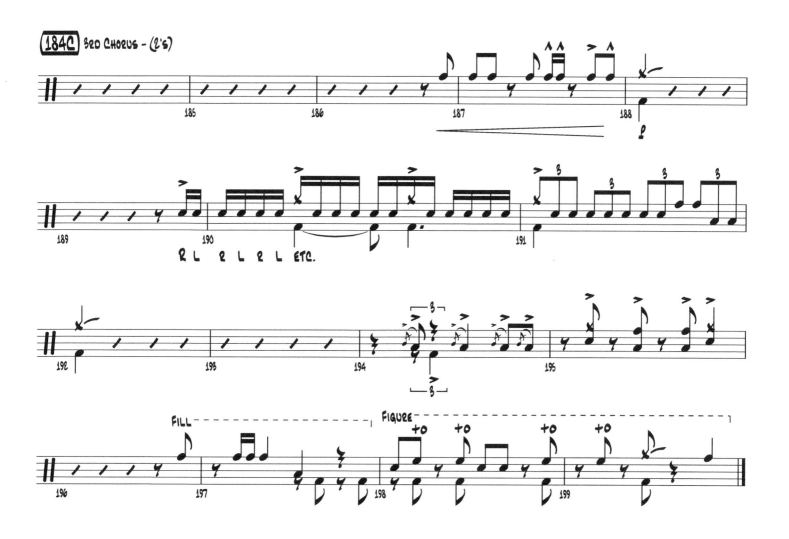